In the beginning…

A cultural commentary on Genesis 1-11

Prof. Tom Meyer

Jerusalem University College

ON THE RECOMMENDATION OF THE FACULTY
AND BY VIRTUE OF THE AUTHORITY VESTED IN THEM
THE BOARD OF DIRECTORS OF JERUSALEM UNIVERSITY COLLEGE
HAVE CONFERRED ON

Thomas Mitchell Meyer

THE DEGREE OF
Master of Arts

IN

MIDDLE EASTERN CULTURES AND RELIGIONS

AND HAVE GRANTED THIS DIPLOMA AS EVIDENCE THEREOF
GIVEN IN THE CITY OF JERUSALEM IN THE STATE OF ISRAEL
UNDER ITS CHARTER FROM THE STATE OF MINNESOTA IN THE UNITED STATES OF AMERICA
ON THE EIGHTH DAY OF OCTOBER IN THE YEAR OF OUR LORD TWO THOUSAND TEN

Dr. Herbert Jacobsen, Chairman of the Board of Directors

Dr. Paul Wright, President

Table of Contents

Introduction   1

Chapter 1   3

Chapter 2   8

Chapter 3   13

Chapter 4   17

Chapter 5   20

Chapter 6   23

Chapter 7   27

Chapter 8   30

Chapter 9   34

Chapter 10   37

Chapter 11   40

❧ *Introduction* ❧

In the beginning is a cultural commentary on Genesis 1-11 written and edited by Prof. Tom Meyer. It attempts to treat the entire foundation of our Christian faith on a verse by verse basis seen through a Middle Eastern cultural lens. I have presented the results of my own careful, personal Bible study and lengthy exposure to Jewish thought and practice while living in Israel the last four years. I have also memorized the entire section and feel I have great contributions and insights to offer the Bible student. For the convenience of the reader, the King James version is used, all Biblical phraseology appears in bold face type, as do all the Biblical verse numbers. The basic aim of this commentary is to determine the meaning of the foundation of our faith. It is therefore, strictly speaking, neither a devotional nor a technical exegetical treatment. It seeks to present the Biblical message in such a way that the Bible student, whether a novice or serious will find extensive explanation, illumination and clarification within its pages.

❧ *Genesis 1* ❧

[1]In the beginning God created the heaven and the earth.

In the first two days of creation Moses describes God and his creation with language that reminds us of the tent dwelling Patriarchs that dominate the narrative of Genesis. Later Isaiah describes the creation as a Bedouin style tent that encompasses a large family: "It is he that sitteth upon the circle of the earth, and the inhabitants thereof are as grasshoppers; that stretcheth out the heavens as a curtain, and spreadeth them out as a tent to dwell in" (Isaiah 40:22). The idea that God is providing a tent to give shelter from the wind that is hovering or moving upon the face of an uninhabitable land in chapter one would be very familiar and comforting for the original audience. The same language is used for God providing shelter for Jacob in an uninhabitable land in Deuteronomy 32: 10-11. When God creates the firmament or canopy on Day Two consider that the original audience could picture the canopy as the roof of their own tent supporting the rain 'waters' above. Moses is speaking to the original audience in language they understand and can relate to.

God first makes himself known by the name of Elohim which is used 3,358 times in the Bible. Elohim is in the plural form and invites us to consider the Trinitarian God in the very first words of the Bible. Certainly Elohim is one God as the Shema says in Deuteronomy 6:4. My rabbinic teacher in Jerusalem suggests translating the passage in Deuteronomy 6:4 as "The Lord our God is unified (one)." Since the Rabbis do not believe in the deity of Yeshua or the Holy Spirit they erroneously explain away mentions of Elohim in the plural as representing God the Father and the angels he created, but they encounter the first of many hermeneutical problem when Elohim says let us create man.

[2]And the earth was without form, and void; and darkness was upon the face of the deep. And the Spirit of God moved upon the face of the waters.

Please recall as we progress through these early chapters that darkness and not light is first mentioned in the Bible. The picture in the verse is of the Holy Spirit hovering or fluttering across the deep. This is the same idea the same author uses in his famous song in Deuteronomy 32: 11. According to Hebrew tradition the song of Moses is one of the eleven great songs in the Bible. Those songs are Psalm 92 a song of the Sabbath, Exodus 15 the song of Miriam, Numbers 21:17 the Song of Israel in the wanderings, Deuteronomy 32 the song of Moses, Joshua 12 the song of the Sun and Moon, Judges 5 the song of Deborah, 1 Samuel 2 the song of Hannah, 2 Samuel 22 the song of David, the Song of Songs which is Solomon's and finally the Song of the Lamb in Revelation 15.

[3]And God said, Let there be light: and there was light.

The sense of the spoken word as divine power is especially vivid in the foundational accounts of diverse peoples, ancient and modern, in all parts of the world but especially in the ancient near east. Accounts of the origin of the world ascribe the initial creative act to the spoken divine word, not only in the opening of Genesis but also the Gospel of John (In the beginning was the Word…). As we shall observe in the rest of the Scriptures the power to bless and curse, create and destroy was recognized by the ancients in the power of the spoken word.

⁴And God saw the light, that it was good: and God divided the light from the darkness. ⁵And God called the light Day, and the darkness he called Night. And the evening and the morning were the first day.

The pattern of evening and morning begins here and traces its way throughout the Scriptures. Eschatologically speaking the day of the Lord with "darkness, gloominess, clouds, and thick darkness" (Zephaniah 1:15) comes first, then the heavenly light comes "for the Lord God gives them light and they shall reign forever and ever" (Revelation 22:5). In other words, the darkness of the seven year tribulation comes first then the light of the millennial kingdom will come.

⁶And God said, Let there be a firmament in the midst of the waters, and let it divide the waters from the waters.

The Hebrew word for firmament means an expanse. So we can imagine a stretched out body of water above the heaven that later opened its windows and rained upon the earth for 40 days and 40 nights.

⁷And God made the firmament, and divided the waters which were under the firmament from the waters which were above the firmament: and it was so.

The waters under the firmament are bodies of water upon the earth such as seas and lakes, and the waters above are the canopy or expanse of water stored up for the judgment of the flood.

⁸And God called the firmament Heaven. And the evening and the morning were the second day.

The literal reading in Hebrew is "it was evening and morning day two." Traditionally the Hebrew day starts when the sun has set and three stars are observed in the heavens.

⁹And God said, Let the waters under the heaven be gathered together unto one place, and let the dry land appear: and it was so. ¹⁰And God called the dry land Earth; and the gathering together of the waters called he Seas: and God saw that it was good.

Whereas Adam later names the creatures he has dominion over, Elohim first names the earth and the sea thereby publicly proclaiming ownership over them.

¹¹And God said, Let the earth bring forth grass, the herb yielding seed, and the fruit tree yielding fruit after his kind, whose seed is in itself, upon the earth: and it was so. ¹²And the earth brought forth grass, and herb yielding seed after his kind, and the tree yielding fruit, whose seed was in itself, after his kind: and God saw that it was good.

"After their kind" does not suggest change or chance but future reproduction of the original created mature trees, herbs, etc. exactly after the pattern of the progenitor.

¹³And the evening and the morning were the third day.

Interestingly we have the order of creation exactly the opposite from the religion of evolution. We miraculously have the creation of plant life before the creation of the sun needed to feed them.

¹⁴And God said, Let there be lights in the firmament of the heaven to divide the day from the night; and let them be for signs, and for seasons, and for days, and years:

The heavenly bodies are to be daily reminders of the creator's handiwork and to serve as the basis for calendars such as the Hebrew's use of the lunar calendar. Over time men in the ancient near east turned the stars good intention into evil and began to fear falling stars, eclipses and solar activities (Jeremiah 10:2).

¹⁵And let them be for lights in the firmament of the heaven to give light upon the earth: and it was so. ¹⁶And God made two great lights; the greater light to rule the day, and the lesser light to rule the night: he made the stars also.

The moon is not a light but a reflector of light. We must keep in mind that even though the text is inspired the author was at times limited to their own personality, education, characteristics and background when trying to convey the meaning behind scientifically oriented subjects to their original audience. Later in the Psalms we read that not only is Elohim so great and powerful to create but he has even numbered and named all the stars in the galaxy (Psalm 147:3).

¹⁷And God set them in the firmament of the heaven to give light upon the earth,

Elohim deliberately fixed or placed the stars where he wanted them. If the sun were 92 million miles away the earth would be consumed with fire and if it were 94 million miles away the earth would freeze. But because our God's wisdom is infinite he placed it precisely at 93 million miles away so we can have spring time and harvest, cold and heat, and summer and winter.

¹⁸And to rule over the day and over the night, and to divide the light from the darkness: and God saw that it was good. ¹⁹And the evening and the morning were the fourth day.

²⁰And God said, Let the waters bring forth abundantly the moving creature that hath life, and fowl that may fly above the earth in the open firmament of heaven. ²¹And God created great whales, and every living creature that moveth, which the waters brought forth abundantly, after their kind, and every winged fowl after his kind: and God saw that it was good.

The Hebrew word *tanniym* does not necessarily mean a whale as in shamoo. The word means a dragon and is used 21 times in the Tenach from Genesis to Malachi. In this context it is a marine monster or sea dragon like the Leviathan (Job 41). In other contexts the same word refers to a land monster or dragon (Malachi 1:3).

²²And God blessed them, saying, Be fruitful, and multiply, and fill the waters in the seas, and let fowl multiply in the earth.

This is the first time that Elohim blesses his creation. We can also consider this the first of the 6,468 commands in the Bible.

²³And the evening and the morning were the fifth day.

²⁴And God said, Let the earth bring forth the living creature after his kind, cattle, and creeping thing, and beast of the earth after his kind: and it was so.²⁵And God made the beast of the earth after his kind, and cattle after their kind, and every thing that creepeth upon the earth after his kind: and God saw that it was good. ²⁶And God said, Let us make man in our image, after our likeness: and let them have dominion over the fish of the sea, and over the fowl of the air, and over the cattle, and over all the earth, and over every creeping thing that creepeth upon the earth. ²⁷So God created man in his own image, in the image of God created he him; male and female created he them.

The word for image in Hebrew is *zelen* and in Greek it is *icon*. This image is imprinted on every soul and cannot be darkened or perverted by sin. In chapter nine of Genesis it says "in the image of God made he man." But can the likeness of God be darkened or perverted by sin? Are there any other places in the Bible after the creation account were image and likenesses are linked together again? Are there any verses stating that man is made in God's likeness after the fall?

²⁸And God blessed them, and God said unto them, Be fruitful, and multiply, and replenish the earth, and subdue it: and have dominion over the fish of the sea, and over the fowl of the air, and over every living thing that moveth upon the earth.

The economy of the ancient near eastern world was dedicated to the two basic resources of land and family. These are the two most important aspects of society and the measure by which someone was valued. This is also to a great extent the case today in Israel. Therefore it should be to no surprise that of the 613 different commandments in the Torah 212 of them can be applied to the development of land and family matters.

Replenish is a faulty translation. The Hebrew word means to fill not to refill as the KJV expresses. This is because some of the translators of the KJV adhered to the erroneous Gap Theory last century. The Gap Theory does not rest on solid exegetical grounds. The fact that it became popular around the same time as the religion of evolution came on the scene makes one suspect that it gained acceptance among evangelicals because it easily accommodates the apparent findings of evolution. In short, the Gap Theory believes that God began to create on 1:1 and then rested for millennia until 1:2. In the time between those two verses the world became a graveyard of dinosaurs and man and then Elohim recreated everything again in seven days.

²⁹And God said, Behold, I have given you every herb bearing seed, which is upon the face of all the earth, and every tree, in the which is the fruit of a tree yielding seed; to you it shall be for meat.

This is the first time the word "behold" is used. The Hebrew word *hine* and the Greek word *edu* appear 1326 times in 1275 different verses. The word behold is a literary device that strives to reel in the attention of the hearer or reader and prepare them for something significant to be spoken.

³⁰And to every beast of the earth, and to every fowl of the air, and to every thing that creepeth upon the earth, wherein there is life, I have given every green herb for meat: and it was so.

Green is the first color mentioned in the Bible.

³¹And God saw every thing that he had made, and, behold, it was very good. And the evening and the morning were the sixth day.

❧ *Genesis 2* ❧

¹Thus the heavens and the earth were finished, and all the host of them.

Though we are thankful that the system of chapter divisions was introduced in 1238 C.E. by Cardinal Hugo de S. Caro and verse notations were added in 1551 by Robertus Stephanus after the advent of the printing press their divisions are not always excellent. This is the first of very few examples of a bad chapter break. Chapter one ought to end after 2:3. A later example is Isaiah 52:13 which ought to be the opening verse of Isaiah 53.

²And on the seventh day God ended his work which he had made; and he rested on the seventh day from all his work which he had made.

It is unusual that there is no evening and morning formula on day seven. The seven day week the Israelites were now instituting would have been extraordinary coming out of a 10 day "week" in Egypt, and the notion of resting on one of the seven days to honor God would have been foolishness to the world but unto the Jews who were saved the Sabbath was the power of God.

³And God blessed the seventh day, and sanctified it: because that in it he had rested from all his work which God created and made.

This verse should be considered the last verse of chapter one, to not divide the chapter here takes away from the ebb and flow of the narrative.

⁴These are the generations of the heavens and of the earth when they were created, in the day that the LORD God made the earth and the heavens,

This is the first time that the divine compound name YHWH Elohim appears. Since it is not exactly known how to pronounce the divine name, (vowel points were not introduced into the Hebrew text until the Masoratic period around the 3ʳᵈ century C.E.) Jews today have constructed a fence around the divine name in order to protect it's sanctity by instead calling YHWH the name of Hashem which translated means "The Name."

⁵And every plant of the field before it was in the earth, and every herb of the field before it grew: for the LORD God had not caused it to rain upon the earth, and there was not a man to till the ground.

These plants of the field seem to be created outside the borders of the garden and in fact were planted before the garden itself. The fields and plants are located in are the same fields that Adam and his sons will later till outside the garden (Genesis 4:12).

⁶But there went up a mist from the earth, and watered the whole face of the ground.

When you read the text and come across the word "dew" think of temperature control. There is no rain in Israel from May to August so dew becomes the sustaining life force for the plants of the field.

⁷And the LORD God formed man of the dust of the ground, and breathed into his nostrils the breath of life; and man became a living soul.

The LORD God formed three things by his breath: Scripture (2 Timothy 3:16), the heavens and all the host of them (Psalm 33:6), and man (Genesis 2.7).

⁸And the LORD God planted a garden eastward in Eden; and there he put the man whom he had formed.

When you come across the geographical indicator east or eastward in Scripture, more often than not it symbolizes judgment or pending judgment. Elsewhere in Genesis the notion of eastward is associated with judgment and separation from God (3:24, 11:2, 13:11). As you read through Scripture you observe the glory departing from Jerusalem to the east (Ezekiel 11:23) and the Messiah's foot standing upon the Mount of Olives to the East at the second coming (Zechariah 14:4). These are just a few of the many eastern indicators we will observe.

Eden means delight in Hebrew or Edin in Akkadian means a geographical plain. The garden like the future tabernacle and temple was the only place where man could enjoy the fellowship and presence of Elohim.

Let us also observe that the creator of the seven days has now taken the form of a man or a gardener. As we shall see in chapter three the gardener, the Lord God, walks in his garden. This is the same Lord God, the same gardener that later appeared to Mary Magdalene in Jerusalem after his resurrection in John 20:15: "Jesus saith unto her, Woman, why weepest thou? Whom seekest thou? She, supposing him to be the gardener..." The gardener/LORD God that planted and walked in Eden was the pre-incarnate Jesus Christ.

⁹And out of the ground made the LORD God to grow every tree that is pleasant to the sight, and good for food; the tree of life also in the midst of the garden, and the tree of knowledge of good and evil.

The gardener is maintaining his garden and instructing Adam his son how to do the same. Later in the account he commands Adam to dress or maintain the garden He planted and to guard it.

¹⁰And a river went out of Eden to water the garden; and from thence it was parted, and became into four heads.

The rivers are geographical boundary markers for Eden, the dwelling place of Elohim. Here we have the first of many boundary lines ordained by Elohim.

¹¹The name of the first is Pison: that is it which compasseth the whole land of Havilah, where there is gold;

Pison is to be identified in Saudi Arabia.

¹²And the gold of that land is good: there is bdellium and the onyx stone. ¹³And the name of the second river is Gihon: the same is it that compasseth the whole land of Ethiopia.

Many rabbis identify Jerusalem as the site of the Garden of Eden. The rabbis use the river Gihon as being one in the same with the Gihon spring whose origin is in the Kidron Valley at the foot of the city of David. On a different note the translation Ethiopia is more correctly Cush.

¹⁴And the name of the third river is Hiddekel: that is it which goeth toward the east of Assyria. And the fourth river is Euphrates.

Hiddekel is the ancient name of the Tigris River.

¹⁵And the LORD God took the man, and put him into the Garden of Eden to dress it and to keep it.

The garden was the first abode of YHWH where he dwelt with his people. The second was the tabernacle and the third was the temple in Jerusalem. All of these homes of YHWH were oriented towards the east and those who ministered therein where all instructed to literally do the same thing; to dress/maintain and guard the house of God. So we have to ask ourselves who is Adam to guard the garden from? The snake?

Also all of these abodes of God had only one way in and one way out and were all oriented to the east. This is the beginning of their being only one way to God.

¹⁶And the LORD God commanded the man, saying, Of every tree of the garden thou mayest freely eat:

This is the first time it explicitly says that YHWH Elohim commanded man with an instruction.

It is interesting how Moses evaluates man's continuing relationship with his Lord by means of eating food (later we read "and when he had dipped the bread he gave it to Judas Iscariot"). Later it is exactly over the issue of eating food that the serpent raises concerns about God's concern for Adam and the woman.

¹⁷But of the tree of the knowledge of good and evil, thou shalt not eat of it: for in the day that thou eatest thereof thou shalt surely die.

This is the beginning of man choosing to go through the narrow or wide gate. If man obeys the Word of the Lord he shall live if he seeks wisdom apart from the Word of the Lord he shall die. See Deuteronomy 30:15-18.

¹⁸And the LORD God said, It is not good that the man should be alone; I will make him an help meet for him.

YHWH Elohim knows what is good. He will build a "mirrored image" of the man.

[19] And out of the ground the LORD God formed every beast of the field, and every fowl of the air; and brought them unto Adam to see what he would call them: and whatsoever Adam called every living creature, that was the name thereof.

The act of naming the animals is the first recorded human activity.

[20] And Adam gave names to all cattle, and to the fowl of the air, and to every beast of the field; but for Adam there was not found an help meet for him.

This is a picture of Adam searching for a partner. The Babylonian Talmud Yebamoth 63a states that Adam had sexual intercourse with all the animals of the garden and only then realized he could not find a helper suitable for him. This is a perfect example of how man attempts to seek wisdom apart from the written Word of God and erroneously claim their own words as divine. The rabbis like the cults and the serpent have broadened thus saith the Lord to encompass non-Biblical texts. This is the beginning of sorrows.

[21] And the LORD God caused a deep sleep to fall upon Adam, and he slept: and he took one of his ribs, and closed up the flesh instead thereof;

The phrase relating to man falling into a "deep sleep" also appears in Genesis 15:12 and Daniel 8:18. When we can connect the literary dots of repeated phrases like this we conclude that whenever a deep sleep falls upon a saint some divinely ordained action or information will be conveyed to them.

[22] And the rib, which the LORD God had taken from man, made he a woman, and brought her unto the man.

The picture is of a wedding procession. The gardener, the Lord God is bringing his daughter to Adam to wed. Elohim did not take the woman out of the man's foot, then he would think he could step over her, and he did not take her out of his head, for then he would think he was mentally superior than her, Elohim took her out of his side so they could walk together agreed side by side.

[23] And Adam said, This is now bone of my bones, and flesh of my flesh: she shall be called Woman, because she was taken out of Man.

The creation account ends with a short poetic discourse.

[24] Therefore shall a man leave his father and his mother, and shall cleave unto his wife: and they shall be one flesh.

Interestingly the Biblical pattern for marriage is to leave your family and cleave to your spouse. Leaving our parents means being willing to give up our own man made traditions regarding family structure and function, if those traditions are not commanded by Scripture. Leaving your parents does not mean that children stop honoring their parents. Leaving means certain aspects of the parent-child relationship before marriage must be put off after marriage because their relationship is forever altered by their marriage.

[25]And they were both naked, the man and his wife, and were not ashamed.

This statement is linking the blessing of the wife and nakedness with the fall.

❧ *Genesis 3* ❧

¹Now the serpent was more subtil than any beast of the field which the LORD God had made. And he said unto the woman, Yea, hath God said, Ye shall not eat of every tree of the garden?

Is this beast of the field first pictured outside of the Garden of Eden? Does he slither his way into the camp when Adam was supposed to be keeping the way? The motif of the enemy slithering into the camp was also used by the author of Joshua when he describers the Gibeonites journey from the Central Benjamin Plateau into the camp of Israel at Gilgal. Because the Israelites were not guarding their abode like Adam, the Gibeonites who like the serpent altered their outward appearance tricked the man Joshua into believing their lie and of course a fall like scenario soon occurred after the event in Joshua.

²And the woman said unto the serpent, We may eat of the fruit of the trees of the garden: ³But of the fruit of the tree which is in the midst of the garden, God hath said, Ye shall not eat of it, neither shall ye touch it, lest ye die.

Within the words of Eve we have an example of Judaism's practice of putting a hedge around the Torah. Elohim did not tell Adam he could not touch it. Yet, Adam in his love for the woman put a fence of protection around the commandment in order to be extra sure she would not transgress the Word of God.

⁴And the serpent said unto the woman, Ye shall not surely die: ⁵For God doth know that in the day ye eat thereof, then your eyes shall be opened, and ye shall be as gods, knowing good and evil.

So begins the ministry of the father of lies (John 8:44). The snake suggests that Elohim is keeping knowledge or what is good from his children. So the woman begins the quest for wisdom and "the good" apart from the Word of God. She thinks God's Word is not the final authority and must go outside those holy parameters to find what is Truth.

⁶And when the woman saw that the tree was good for food, and that it was pleasant to the eyes, and a tree to be desired to make one wise, she took of the fruit thereof, and did eat, and gave also unto her husband with her; and he did eat.

The phrase "when the woman saw that the tree was good" should be compared with the previous statements that "God saw that it was good." Only God knows what is good, namely his Word. The motif of see, take, and give is also repeated throughout the Scriptures. Take the example of Samson "and he saw and behold there was a swarm of bees and honey in the carcass of the lion and he took in his hand and did eat and gave to his father and mother and they did eat" (Judges 14:9). This motif is also expressed by John "for all that is in the world, the lust of the flesh, and the lust of the eyes, and the pride of life" (1 John 2:16). This is the age old adage of trying to justify our actions by reasoning that our way is better than the way expressed in the Word of God.

[7]And the eyes of them both were opened, and they knew that they were naked; and they sewed fig leaves together, and made themselves aprons.

They now knew they were naked in the sense of being under Elohim's judgment. The word for sewing is to portray a well crafted meticulous garment, not something haphazardly crafted.

[8]And they heard the voice of the LORD God walking in the garden in the cool of the day: and Adam and his wife hid themselves from the presence of the LORD God amongst the trees of the garden.

The Lord God, the Gardener would daily walk in the garden in fellowship with his children. This would take place in the "wind" or cool of the day. This is the time in Jerusalem when dusk arrives and a cool breeze can be expected from the Mediterranean Sea.

The wife still does not yet have a name, but hides with Adam to cover their own sin by their own works.

[9]And the LORD God called unto Adam, and said unto him, Where art thou?

Here we have a courtroom trial scene. In this section we have Elohim as the judge, jury, and executioner in good rabbinic fashion first asking a question. Elohim asks four questions in this trial and then submits the verdict.

[10]And he said, I heard thy voice in the garden, and I was afraid, because I was naked; and I hid myself.

Adam who is on the stand, is convicted by his own words when he acknowledges being naked.

[11]And he said, Who told thee that thou wast naked? Hast thou eaten of the tree, whereof I commanded thee that thou shouldest not eat? [12]And the man said, The woman whom thou gavest to be with me, she gave me of the tree, and I did eat.

This is to be interpreted as Adam viewing the gift from Elohim, the woman, as the source of his trouble. It is Elohim's fault, who is the source of every good and perfect gift, accuses the man.

[13]And the LORD God said unto the woman, What is this that thou hast done? And the woman said, The serpent beguiled me, and I did eat.

The woman likely points up into a tree as she identifies the adversary.

[14]And the LORD God said unto the serpent, Because thou hast done this, thou art cursed above all cattle, and above every beast of the field; upon thy belly shalt thou go, and dust shalt thou eat all the days of thy life:

Here begins the verdict of the trial. The serpent moved upon four legs or amongst the trees in the air before this day. For now it must live on its belly. "And dust shalt thou eat" is to be interpreted as total defeat. Other examples of eating dust as being considered total defeat are Joshua putting his foot on the head of the five Canaanite kings (Joshua 10:25), and David standing upon the head of the Philistine (1 Samuel 17:51).

15And I will put enmity between thee and the woman, and between thy seed and her seed; it shall bruise thy head, and thou shalt bruise his heel.

A book could be written upon this verse alone. In short this begins the battle of the seed of the woman and the seed of the serpent culminating with the destruction of the Serpent at the end of the 1000 year kingdom of Christ (Revelation 20). The seed of the serpent is always trying to eliminate the seed of the woman from which the Messiah will come because the serpent knows that Jesus the Messiah will crush his head shortly (Romans 16:20). Hence Cain kills Abel trying to eliminate the godly line, the sons of God overtake the daughters of men with the same motive, Elohim destroys all the seeds of the serpent and only Noah the seed of the woman is left alive, Pharaoh a seed of the serpent eliminates the seed of the woman by casting the baby boys into the river, and Herod attempts to destroy all the baby boys in the hill of country of Judah 1500 years later. These are just a few of the many obvious and dormant examples of the battle of the seed of the woman and the seed of the serpent culminating in the Apocalypse. This is why Joshua puts his foot on the head of the five Canaanite kings (Joshua 10:25), Jael crushes the head of Sisera (Judges 4:21), and David cuts off the head of Goliath (1 Samuel 17:51).

16Unto the woman he said, I will greatly multiply thy sorrow and thy conception; in sorrow thou shalt bring forth children; and thy desire shall be to thy husband, and he shall rule over thee.

Let us keep in mind that birth pangs are not merely a reminder of the judgment of the fall, they are also a sign of impending joy in the coming kingdom (Romans 8:22-24/ Matthew 24:8).

17And unto Adam he said, Because thou hast hearkened unto the voice of thy wife, and hast eaten of the tree, of which I commanded thee, saying, Thou shalt not eat of it: cursed is the ground for thy sake; in sorrow shalt thou eat of it all the days of thy life;

This shows a reversal of the state of the land being "very good."

18Thorns also and thistles shall it bring forth to thee; and thou shalt eat the herb of the field;

Thorns are now the symbol of the curse. Is it not peculiar that the next time thorns appear in the Bible are in the narrative of the burning thorn (*sineh*) bush (Exodus 3:2). This means that the Lord is beginning to associate himself with the curse and redemption. It should be no surprise that later this symbol of everything unholy, this crown of thorns, is put upon the head of the Son of Man, the seed of the woman who takes away the sins of the world (Matthew 27:29).

19In the sweat of thy face shalt thou eat bread, till thou return unto the ground; for out of it wast thou taken: for dust thou art, and unto dust shalt thou return.

The rabbis say that this is the day Elohim taught man how to make bread.

20And Adam called his wife's name Eve; because she was the mother of all living.

This is the second time Adam named his helper. The first name pointed to her origin and the second to her destiny. She is the mother of all living.

21Unto Adam also and to his wife did the LORD God make coats of skins, and clothed them.

Elohim is back to work. The firstlings of the flock were sacrificed and the innocent blood was shed so man could once again have communion with Elohim. The theme of Elohim working on behalf of the seed of the woman is going to be further developed in the rest of the book and realized in full in the birth of Christ, who is the seed from eternity past.

22And the LORD God said, Behold, the man is become as one of us, to know good and evil: and now, lest he put forth his hand, and take also of the tree of life, and eat, and live for ever:

"One of us" Of course the rabbis misinterpret these passages and appoint them to YHWH and his consortium of angels. This is because they do err, not knowing the Scriptures nor the power of Yeshua the Messiah.

23Therefore the LORD God sent him forth from the garden of Eden, to till the ground from whence he was taken. 24So he drove out the man; and he placed at the east of the garden of Eden Cherubims, and a flaming sword which turned every way, to keep the way of the tree of life.

The Cherubim's guarded the presence of God as did the two angels on the mercy seat of the Ark of the Covenant (Exodus 25:20), and as the two angels outside the tomb of Jesus Christ (John 20:12). In every case, the angels are guarding (like Adam was assigned to do) the presence and glory of God. The angels protected the only way into the Garden of Eden probably until the day that Noah entered the ark. Again let us not forget the geographical direction of eastward often associated with judgment.

ᚙ *Genesis 4* ᚙ

[1]And Adam knew Eve his wife; and she conceived, and bare Cain, and said, I have gotten a man from the LORD.

The reader is in suspense to know if this seed conceived is the seed that will crush the head of the serpent or the seed of the serpent. The English translation is not clear, for it should read "I have gotten a man the Lord." The Hebrew makes it certain that Eve expects this firstborn to be the Messiah figure who will crush the head of the snake. The name Cain means a spear.

[2]And she again bare his brother Abel. And Abel was a keeper of sheep, but Cain was a tiller of the ground.

The name Abel means vapor. Abel is the first prophet though it does not attribute that title to him here in Genesis (Matthew 23:35). It is interesting that the two primary classes of future Israelite society, the shepherd and the farmer are first epitomized here in the beginning. The descendent through which the holy seed and Messiah will come is not the ancient near eastern cultural norm, that is to say the heir apparent or eldest son, but the one whom YHWH chooses.

[3]And in process of time it came to pass, that Cain brought of the fruit of the ground an offering unto the LORD.

This is the first mention of the word "time" in the text.

[4]And Abel, he also brought of the firstlings of his flock and of the fat thereof. And the LORD had respect unto Abel and to his offering:

Why did Elohim have respect unto Abel and not Cain? We know from Leviticus that Elohim accepts both grain and meat sacrifices. The answer is "I desire mercy and not sacrifice, and the knowledge of God more than burnt offerings" (Hosea 6:6). Why do we do what we do?

[5]But unto Cain and to his offering he had not respect. And Cain was very wroth, and his countenance fell. [6]And the LORD said unto Cain, Why art thou wroth? and why is thy countenance fallen? [7]If thou doest well, shalt thou not be accepted? and if thou doest not well, sin lieth at the door. And unto thee shall be his desire, and thou shalt rule over him.

Sin is like a roaring lion crouching at the door to devour Cain. Can Cain face the consequences of premeditated murder and being exiled from the land, exiled like his father Adam?

[8]And Cain talked with Abel his brother: and it came to pass, when they were in the field, that Cain rose up against Abel his brother, and slew him.

Is this the same field (Genesis 3:1) the serpent lived in before he slithered into the garden? The rabbis believe that Cain slew Abel with a field stone but if we take the meaning of their names into consideration Cain slew Abel with a spear.

⁹And the LORD said unto Cain, Where is Abel thy brother? And he said, I know not: Am I my brother's keeper?

Again, Elohim confronts man in good rabbinic fashion, with a question. And in good rabbinic fashion Cain responds with a question.

¹⁰And he said, What hast thou done? The voice of thy brother's blood crieth unto me from the ground. ¹¹And now art thou cursed from the earth, which hath opened her mouth to receive thy brother's blood from thy hand; ¹²When thou tillest the ground, it shall not henceforth yield unto thee her strength; a fugitive and a vagabond shalt thou be in the earth.

"The earth opened her mouth." Here is one of the over 700 quotes or allusions to the Tenach that John uses in the Apocalypse. John wrote in Revelation 12:16 "and the earth helped the woman *and opened her mouth* and swallowed up the flood which the dragon cast out of his mouth." In both instances we have the earth assisting the persecuted seed of the woman.

¹³And Cain said unto the LORD, My punishment is greater than I can bear. ¹⁴Behold, thou hast driven me out this day from the face of the earth; and from thy face shall I be hid; and I shall be a fugitive and a vagabond in the earth; and it shall come to pass, that every one that findeth me shall slay me.

This should be interpreted as an expression of remorse.

¹⁵And the LORD said unto him, Therefore whosoever slayeth Cain, vengeance shall be taken on him sevenfold. And the LORD set a mark upon Cain, lest any finding him should kill him.

Is this mark the predecessor for the mark of the beast? Cain's offense was punishable by death after the time of Noah but apparently not before (Genesis 9:6). Cain is being protected from the cycle of vengeance and the city was likely a prototype of the later cities of refuge.

¹⁶And Cain went out from the presence of the LORD, and dwelt in the land of Nod, on the east of Eden.

Again we have the geographical indicator of east being mentioned within the context of divine judgment. The land of Nod could be translated the land of "wandering". Therefore the imagery of Elohim's judgment against Cain appears to have become a metaphor to the prophets in picturing the judgment of Elohim against his people in their wanderings or exile from the land.

¹⁷And Cain knew his wife; and she conceived, and bare Enoch: and he builded a city, and called the name of the city, after the name of his son, Enoch.

The following names and places reflect the culture which developed in the context of this first city and genealogy.

¹⁸And unto Enoch was born Irad: and Irad begat Mehujael: and Mehujael begat Methusael: and Methusael begat Lamech.

Names in Hebrew often reflect information about the person. This genealogy of the seed of the serpent has men named Irad (fugitive), Mehujael (smitten of God), and Lamech (wild man).

¹⁹And Lamech took unto him two wives: the name of the one was Adah, and the name of the other Zillah. ²⁰And Adah bare Jabal: he was the father of such as dwell in tents, and of such as have cattle.

"Moving" is a fitting name for the man who is the father of those who are sheep and goat people.

²¹And his brother's name was Jubal: he was the father of all such as handle the harp and organ.

"Playing" is a fitting name for the man who is the father of music and arts.

²²And Zillah, she also bare Tubalcain, an instructer of every artificer in brass and iron: and the sister of Tubalcain was Naamah.

"The smith" or Tubalcain is a fitting name for the man who is the father of craftsmanship and the originator of cutting instruments. These descendents in the line of the seed of the serpent are seven generations removed from father Adam.

²³And Lamech said unto his wives, Adah and Zillah, Hear my voice; ye wives of Lamech, hearken unto my speech: for I have slain a man to my wounding, and a young man to my hurt.

This is to be understood as a poetical discourse. The "wild man" composes a curse confessing his two accounts of murder.

²⁴If Cain shall be avenged sevenfold, truly Lamech seventy and sevenfold.

A better translation might be seventy times seven. Christ takes the well known curse of Lamech and turns the saying upon its head to make a blessing out of the well known statement (Matthew 18:21-22). Christ was speaking to his audience in language they understood, memorized Torah language.

²⁵And Adam knew his wife again; and she bare a son, and called his name Seth: For God, said she, hath appointed me another seed instead of Abel, whom Cain slew.

Seth is the heir of the godly seed not his older brother Cain. The pattern of the younger ruling over the older is first established in Genesis 4 and is repeated in the stories of Ishmael and Isaac, Esau and Jacob, and Reuben and Joseph to name a few.

²⁶And to Seth, to him also there was born a son; and he called his name Enos: then began men to call upon the name of the LORD.

Only when two or three were first gathered together in his name did man begin to call upon the name of YHWH.

✑ *Genesis 5* ✑

¹This is the book of the generations of Adam. In the day that God created man, in the likeness of God made he him;

Consider this chapter the beginning of a seam and Genesis 9:29 the other end of the seam. This chapter is a summary of Elohim's plan of salvation, hidden within a genealogy in the beginning of the Torah.

²Male and female created he them; and blessed them, and called their name Adam, in the day when they were created.

In Hebrew Adam means man. This is the first name of ten that will lead us to the message of salvation.

³And Adam lived an hundred and thirty years, and begat a son in his own likeness, and after his image; and called his name Seth: ⁴And the days of Adam after he had begotten Seth were eight hundred years: and he begat sons and daughters: ⁵And all the days that Adam lived were nine hundred and thirty years: and he died. ⁶And Seth lived an hundred and five years, and begat Enos:

In Hebrew Seth means appointed. This is the second name of ten; Man, Appointed.

⁷And Seth lived after he begat Enos eight hundred and seven years, and begat sons and daughters: ⁸And all the days of Seth were nine hundred and twelve years: and he died. ⁹And Enos lived ninety years, and begat Cainan:

In Hebrew Enos means mortal. This is the third name of ten; Man, Appointed, Mortal.

¹⁰And Enos lived after he begat Cainan eight hundred and fifteen years, and begat sons and daughters: ¹¹And all the days of Enos were nine hundred and five years: and he died. ¹²And Cainan lived seventy years and begat Mahalaleel:

In Hebrew Cainan means sorrowful. This is the fourth name of ten; Man, Appointed, Mortal, Sorrowful,

¹³And Cainan lived after he begat Mahalaleel eight hundred and forty years, and begat sons and daughters: ¹⁴And all the days of Cainan were nine hundred and ten years: and he died. ¹⁵And Mahalaleel lived sixty and five years, and begat Jared:

In Hebrew Mahalaleel means The Blessed Lord. This is the fifth name of ten; Man, Appointed, Mortal, Sorrowful, The Blessed Lord.

¹⁶And Mahalaleel lived after he begat Jared eight hundred and thirty years, and begat sons and daughters: ¹⁷And all the days of Mahalaleel were eight hundred ninety and five years: and he died. ¹⁸And Jared lived an hundred sixty and two years, and he begat Enoch:

In Hebrew Jared means shall come down. This is the sixth name of ten; Man, Appointed, Mortal, Sorrowful, The Blessed Lord, Shall come down.

¹⁹And Jared lived after he begat Enoch eight hundred years, and begat sons and daughters: ²⁰And all the days of Jared were nine hundred sixty and two years: and he died. ²¹And Enoch lived sixty and five years, and begat Methuselah:

In Hebrew Enoch means teaching. This is the seventh name of ten; Man, Appointed, Mortal, Sorrowful, The Blessed Lord, Shall come down, Teaching.

²²And Enoch walked with God after he begat Methuselah three hundred years, and begat sons and daughters:

It appears with Enoch we have the first of four generations of preachers. It is interesting to note that Enoch likely began his preaching ministry when he was sixty five, for only then did he begin to walk with Elohim.

²³And all the days of Enoch were three hundred sixty and five years: ²⁴And Enoch walked with God: and he was not; for God took him.

That is to say Enoch did not suffer the fate of father Adam. Enoch is the first of three models of faith and trust in the early chapters of Genesis, the other two being Noah (6:9), and Abraham (15:6).

²⁵And Methuselah lived an hundred eighty and seven years, and begat Lamech.

In Hebrew Methuselah means his death shall bring. This is the eighth name of ten; Man, Appointed, Mortal, Sorrowful, The Blessed Lord, Shall come down, Teaching, His death shall bring.

²⁶And Methuselah lived after he begat Lamech seven hundred eighty and two years, and begat sons and daughters:

Methuselah's life was a symbol of Elohim's mercy in destroying the world through the coming flood. The flood could not come until the death of "his death shall bring" the flood.

²⁷And all the days of Methuselah were nine hundred sixty and nine years: and he died. ²⁸And Lamech lived an hundred eighty and two years, and begat a son:

In Hebrew Lamech means despair. This is the ninth name of ten; Man, Appointed, Mortal, Sorrowful, The Blessed Lord, Shall come down, Teaching, His death shall bring, Despair.

²⁹And he called his name Noah, saying, This same shall comfort us concerning our work and toil of our hands, because of the ground which the LORD hath cursed.

In Hebrew Noah means comfort. This is the tenth name and final piece of the name puzzle presenting

22

the Gospel. Man, Appointed, Mortal, Sorrowful, The Blessed Lord, Shall come down, Teaching, His death shall bring, Despair, and Comfort.

[30]And Lamech lived after he begat Noah five hundred ninety and five years, and begat sons and daughters: [31]And all the days of Lamech were seven hundred seventy and seven years: and he died. [32]And Noah was five hundred years old: and Noah begat Shem, Ham, and Japheth.

Were Shem, Ham and Japheth triplets?

❧ *Genesis 6* ❧

¹And it came to pass, when men began to multiply on the face of the earth, and daughters were born unto them,

According to the ages of the men in Genesis chapter five, the events of chapter six would take place 1656 years after creation. We must always take numbers literally from Genesis to Revelation unless the genre or context clearly states otherwise. To not do so is to twist the Scriptures unto your own destruction.

²That the sons of God saw the daughters of men that they were fair; and they took them wives of all which they chose.

Herein we have the second appearance of the pattern to see, to think it was good, and to take. When reading the rest of Scripture remember to use Genesis 1-11 as the foundational pattern and the basis for many motifs found later. Oceans of ink have been spilled on the subject of who are the sons of God and who are the daughters of men. Let us remember to process our interpretation through the filter of what has been previously revealed in the text and what the original audience would have understood them to be. The thread binding the book together so far is the seed of the serpent versus the seed of the woman.

³And the LORD said, My spirit shall not always strive with man, for that he also is flesh: yet his days shall be an hundred and twenty years.

Does this mean man's life expectancy will now be 120 like Moses the author? Does this mean that the clock is now ticking and man has 120 years until the flood?

⁴There were giants in the earth in those days; and also after that, when the sons of God came in unto the daughters of men, and they bare children to them, the same became mighty men which were of old, men of renown.

The Hebrew word giant literally means those who tyrannize.

⁵And God saw that the wickedness of man was great in the earth, and that every imagination of the thoughts of his heart was only evil continually. ⁶And it repented the LORD that he had made man on the earth, and it grieved him at his heart. ⁷And the LORD said, I will destroy man whom I have created from the face of the earth; both man, and beast, and the creeping thing, and the fowls of the air; for it repenteth me that I have made them.

"And God saw" this phrase was used often in the beginning of Genesis. The verbal parallels from earlier suggest that Moses intends the two narratives to contrast the welfare of man before and after

24

the exile from Eden.

"Every imagination of his heart…" There is no geographical distance in the Hebrew mind between the mind and the heart, they are one in the same. The heart when considered figuratively is the inner control center of man. Out of it flow all the issues of life (Proverbs 4:23), it is the location of motives and character (Matthew 6:21). It is the portion of man about which Elohim is most concerned (1 Samuel 16:7).

⁸But Noah found grace in the eyes of the LORD.

The term "the eyes of the LORD" occurs 22 times in the Bible. The only New Testament mention is Peter using it to quote the Tenach (Psalm 34:15). It is used in a positive relation nine times in reference to Noah (Genesis 6:8), the Holy Land (Deuteronomy 11:12), the whole earth (2 Chronicles 16:9), man in general (Proverbs 5:21), the righteous (Psalm 34:15), David (1 Samuel 26:24), Asa (1 Kings 15:11), Jehoshaphat (1 Kings 22:43) and Isaiah (Isaiah 49:5).

It is used in a negative relation five times in reference to Omri (1 Kings 16:25) and Jehoram (2 Chronicles 21:6), "our fathers" (2 Chronicles 29:6), the northern kingdom (Amos 9:8), and Zedekiah (Jeremiah 52:2). Can we understand this to also mean that Noah (Comfort) brought comfort to Elohim that all was not lost?

⁹These are the generations of Noah: Noah was a just man and perfect in his generations, and Noah walked with God.

It is interesting to note that Noah is the first to be called a just man. The same explanation for Enoch's rescue from death is made the basis for Noah's rescue from death in the flood, namely they walked with Elohim. Enoch and Noah are the only two recorded people in the Bible to walk with God. It is implied Micah did walk with God after the model of Enoch and Noah and encouraged his contemporaries and us today via application to do the same (Micah 6:8). It seems Jehu is the only person called out personally in the text for not walking in the Torah of the Lord God of Israel (2 Kings 10:31).

¹⁰And Noah begat three sons, Shem, Ham, and Japheth.

Their names mean "Name," "Hot" and "Wide spreading." Of course these names are prophetic of their destiny and their offspring's future as we later see in chapters nine and ten.

¹¹The earth also was corrupt before God, and the earth was filled with violence.

We are to contrast what we just read of Noah being just with the world around him that was filled with violence. Noah is like Lot in that he is the remnant living amidst a soon destroyed world that vexes his righteous soul daily.

We are also to contrast the idea of the earth being "filled" by Adam and Eve in the beginning with the earth now being "filled" with violence by the seed of the serpent.

¹²And God looked upon the earth, and, behold, it was corrupt; for all flesh had corrupted his

way upon the earth. ¹³And God said unto Noah, The end of all flesh is come before me; for the earth is filled with violence through them; and, behold, I will destroy them with the earth.

Of course this verse reminds us of the warning given to Lot and his family before the destruction of Sodom. In the text YHWH never destroys without first warning his people and giving them a way to escape that they might be able to bear it.

¹⁴Make thee an ark of gopher wood; rooms shalt thou make in the ark, and shalt pitch it within and without with pitch.

After the story of Noah the next time the word ark appears is in Exodus chapter two in the account of baby Moses. Another parallel with the Moses story is that not only our both men God's chosen redeemers and are rescued in an ark, but their arks are "pitched" or literally atoned inside and out. This is the only time the word gopher wood is used in the Bible.

¹⁵And this is the fashion which thou shalt make it of: The length of the ark shall be three hundred cubits, the breadth of it fifty cubits, and the height of it thirty cubits.

There is a literary connection between the creation account and the building of the ark. Each passage has a pattern. Elohim speaks, an action is commanded, and the action is executed exactly according to Elohim's will. Each of these accounts culminates with a blessing from heaven.

¹⁶A window shalt thou make to the ark, and in a cubit shalt thou finish it above; and the door of the ark shalt thou set in the side thereof; with lower, second, and third stories shalt thou make it.

It is interesting that there is only one way into the ark just like the tabernacle, the temple, and to the Father (John 14:6).

¹⁷And, behold, I, even I, do bring a flood of waters upon the earth, to destroy all flesh, wherein is the breath of life, from under heaven; and every thing that is in the earth shall die. ¹⁸But with thee will I establish my covenant; and thou shalt come into the ark, thou, and thy sons, and thy wife, and thy sons' wives with thee.

This is the first mention of the word covenant in the Bible. It is used 295 times in total.

¹⁹And of every living thing of all flesh, two of every sort shalt thou bring into the ark, to keep them alive with thee; they shall be male and female. ²⁰Of fowls after their kind, and of cattle after their kind, of every creeping thing of the earth after his kind, two of every sort shall come unto thee, to keep them alive.

The previous verse said that Noah shall bring the animals into the ark and this verse says the animals will come to him. This is not a contradiction but an expression of Hebrew not Greek thinking. This is the same idea as 1 Chronicles 21:1 "And satan stood up against Israel and provoked David to number Israel" and the parallel account in 2 Samuel 24:1 "and again the anger of the Lord was kindled against Israel, and he moved David against them to say, Go number Israel and Judah." These are not contradictions but just two sides of the same Hebrew coin.

26

21And take thou unto thee of all food that is eaten, and thou shalt gather it to thee; and it shall be for food for thee, and for them. 22Thus did Noah; according to all that God commanded him, so did he.

Obedience to the commands of YHWH is the only way to salvation. Later Abram (Genesis 12:4) and the Israelites will be called upon to show evidence of the same lesson like you are today (John 14:15).

❧ *Genesis 7* ❧

¹And the LORD said unto Noah, Come thou and all thy house into the ark; for thee have I seen righteous before me in this generation.

The ark is now finished after 120 years of construction and Noah preaching to that evil and adulterous generation (1 Peter 2:5).

²Of every clean beast thou shalt take to thee by sevens, the male and his female: and of beasts that are not clean by two, the male and his female. ³Of fowls also of the air by sevens, the male and the female; to keep seed alive upon the face of all the earth.

Not only would these animals be fruitful and multiply upon the earth after the flood, but Noah would use these exact animals to offer a sacrifice to YHWH after the flood.

⁴For yet seven days, and I will cause it to rain upon the earth forty days and forty nights; and every living substance that I have made will I destroy from off the face of the earth.

Why seven days wait? I would suggest this to be the time of the death and mourning of Methuselah whose name means "his death shall bring" the flood. We know from later in Genesis that the family of Jacob mourned seven days after his death (Genesis 50:10).

⁵And Noah did according unto all that the LORD commanded him.

Noah, Moses and David are the only ones specifically recognized in the Bible as doing "all that the LORD commanded them."

⁶And Noah was six hundred years old when the flood of waters was upon the earth.

The flood of waters is a reversal of the creation account. We see this same pattern of an undoing of creation later in Zephaniah chapter one when he describes the undoing of creation when YHWH the might warrior returns to judge.

⁷And Noah went in, and his sons, and his wife, and his sons' wives with him, into the ark, because of the waters of the flood.

This is the evidence of the faith of Noah. He had moved with fear and prepared an ark for the saving of his house by which he condemned the world and became heir of the righteousness which is by faith (Hebrews 11:7). This verse was quoted from memory by Christ in Matthew 24:38.

⁸Of clean beasts, and of beasts that are not clean, and of fowls, and of every thing that creepeth upon the earth, ⁹There went in two and two unto Noah into the ark, the male and the female, as

28

God had commanded Noah.

The next time we read about The Lord calling two and two is when Christ sends out his disciples two and two into every city and place where he himself would soon come and preach (Luke 10:1).

¹⁰And it came to pass after seven days, that the waters of the flood were upon the earth.

We can perhaps understand this to mean that the Sabbath of weeping and mourning for Methuselah was over.

¹¹In the six hundredth year of Noah's life, in the second month, the seventeenth day of the month, the same day were all the fountains of the great deep broken up, and the windows of heaven were opened. ¹²And the rain was upon the earth forty days and forty nights.

The number forty appears often in the Bible. The children of Israel ate manna for forty years (Exodus 16:35), Moses was on Mount Horeb forty days (Exodus 24:18), the spies searched the land for forty days (Numbers 13:25), the children of Israel wandered for forty years (Numbers 14:33), the land of Israel rested forty years after the ministry of certain judges (Judges 3:11, 5:31), the land of Israel was delivered into the hand of the Philistines forty years (Judges 13:1), Eli judged Israel forty years (1 Samuel 4:18), Goliath presented himself for forty days (1 Samuel 17:16), David reigned for forty years (1 Kings 2:11), Solomon reigned for forty years (2 Chronicles 9:30), Jonah gave Nineveh forty days to repent (Jonah 3:4), Christ was in the wilderness fasting for forty days (Matthew 4:2), and was seen for forty days after his resurrection (Acts 1:3).

¹³In the selfsame day entered Noah, and Shem, and Ham, and Japheth, the sons of Noah, and Noah's wife, and the three wives of his sons with them, into the ark;

In 1 Peter 3:21, Peter understands the ark to prefigure the saving work of Christ as it is pictured in baptism.

¹⁴They, and every beast after his kind, and all the cattle after their kind, and every creeping thing that creepeth upon the earth after his kind, and every fowl after his kind, every bird of every sort. ¹⁵And they went in unto Noah into the ark, two and two of all flesh, wherein is the breath of life. ¹⁶And they that went in, went in male and female of all flesh, as God had commanded him: and the LORD shut him in.

The only other thing the Lord "shuts" in the Bible is the womb of Hannah (1 Samuel 1:6).

¹⁷And the flood was forty days upon the earth; and the waters increased, and bare up the ark, and it was lift up above the earth. ¹⁸And the waters prevailed, and were increased greatly upon the earth; and the ark went upon the face of the waters. ¹⁹And the waters prevailed exceedingly upon the earth; and all the high hills, that were under the whole heaven, were covered.

Remember that YHWH had not told Noah how long he would be in the ark just how long it would rain.

²⁰Fifteen cubits upward did the waters prevail; and the mountains were covered.

The standard cubit was an ancient near eastern measurement that was the length from the middle finger to the elbow of a grown man. Typically this measurement was 18" but the Royal Cubit was approximately 21". The highest mountain on earth was covered with more than 23' of water.

[21]**And all flesh died that moved upon the earth, both of fowl, and of cattle, and of beast, and of every creeping thing that creepeth upon the earth, and every man:** [22]**All in whose nostrils was the breath of life, of all that was in the dry land, died.**

This verse reminds us of a later narrative in Joshua where a similar execution of the seed of the serpent is taking place. In Genesis Elohim is destroying the seed of the serpent upon all the land and later Joshua is destroying the seed of the serpent upon all the Promised Land.

[23]**And every living substance was destroyed which was upon the face of the ground, both man, and cattle, and the creeping things, and the fowl of the heaven; and they were destroyed from the earth: and Noah only remained alive, and they that were with him in the ark.** [24]**And the waters prevailed upon the earth an hundred and fifty days.**

The waters have already flooded the entire earth for 40 days and have increased for 110 days after the initial 40 days. Noah and his family have been in the ark for five months.

❧ *Genesis 8* ❧

¹And God remembered Noah, and every living thing, and all the cattle that was with him in the ark: and God made a wind to pass over the earth, and the waters assuaged;

To remember in Hebrew is to call to mind a past event with the purpose of evoking some action. We have a picture of a sort of recreation of the earth. As in Genesis chapter one, we have the wind or spirit moving upon the face of the waters.

The author of the Torah is Moses and we should not be surprised to see familiar motifs throughout his five books. Noah's rescue in many accounts foreshadows the Exodus from Egypt. The first parallel is here where Elohim "remembers" as in Exodus 2:24 when Elohim remembers his covenant with Abraham, Isaac and Jacob. A second example is also found here with the mention of the work of the wind on the waters as the east wind parted the Red Sea in Exodus 14:21. In both cases the wind moves upon the water to carry out the salvation of the people of God.

²The fountains also of the deep and the windows of heaven were stopped, and the rain from heaven was restrained; ³And the waters returned from off the earth continually: and after the end of the hundred and fifty days the waters were abated. ⁴And the ark rested in the seventh month, on the seventeenth day of the month, upon the mountains of Ararat.

In Genesis the traditional Jewish calendar is used. It isn't until the first Passover in Exodus that the new calendar is implemented. The seventh month of Genesis becomes the first month of Nisan in Exodus. In the new calendar the ark rested, or the new creation began on the first month, on the seventeenth day of the month. Christ was crucified on Passover, the fourteenth day of the month Nisan. Fourteen days into the month plus three days in the heart of the earth. The day of Christ's resurrection was also on the seventeenth day of the first month. The new beginning of earth in the days of Noah was to occur exactly the same day as the new beginning or the firstborn from the dead, Christ.

⁵And the waters decreased continually until the tenth month: in the tenth month, on the first day of the month, were the tops of the mountains seen.

The waters have now covered the earth for 224 days.

⁶And it came to pass at the end of forty days, that Noah opened the window of the ark which he had made:

The waters have now covered the earth for 264 days.

⁷And he sent forth a raven, which went forth to and fro, until the waters were dried up from

off the earth.

Noah is sending forth spies to gather intelligence. This reminds us of Moses sending out spies into the land for the same purpose (Numbers 13). Some have suggested the black raven and the white dove are symbolic of the Law of Moses and the grace of Jesus Christ.

⁸Also he sent forth a dove from him, to see if the waters were abated from off the face of the ground;

The waters have now covered the earth for 271 days. Noah has been in the ark for over nine months.

⁹But the dove found no rest for the sole of her foot, and she returned unto him into the ark, for the waters were on the face of the whole earth: then he put forth his hand, and took her, and pulled her in unto him into the ark. ¹⁰And he stayed yet other seven days; and again he sent forth the dove out of the ark;

The waters have now covered the earth for 278 days.

¹¹And the dove came in to him in the evening; and, lo, in her mouth was an olive leaf pluckt off: so Noah knew that the waters were abated from off the earth.

The olive tree becomes synonymous with strength and fertility.

¹²And he stayed yet other seven days; and sent forth the dove; which returned not again unto him any more.

The waters have now covered the earth for 285 days.

¹³And it came to pass in the six hundredth and first year, in the first month, the first day of the month, the waters were dried up from off the earth: and Noah removed the covering of the ark, and looked, and, behold, the face of the ground was dry.

Here is a third example of Noah's rescue foreshadowing the Exodus, namely the miracle of dry ground after the work of the wind on the waters and the destruction of the seed of the serpent.

¹⁴And in the second month, on the seven and twentieth day of the month, was the earth dried.

Noah and his family were inside the ark for a total of 371 days.

¹⁵And God spake unto Noah, saying,

The phrase "God spake unto" or 'the Lord spake unto' is only directed towards Noah, Hagar (Genesis 16:13), Israel (Genesis 46:2), Moses (Exodus 6:2), Joshua (Joshua 4:1), Samuel (1 Samuel 9:17) and David (1 Kings 5:5).

¹⁶Go forth of the ark, thou, and thy wife, and thy sons, and thy sons' wives with thee.

Just as Elohim told Noah to go forth so he later tells Abram to go (Gen. 12:1).

[17]Bring forth with thee every living thing that is with thee, of all flesh, both of fowl, and of cattle, and of every creeping thing that creepeth upon the earth; that they may breed abundantly in the earth, and be fruitful, and multiply upon the earth.

This verse follows after the pattern of Genesis chapter one and is pregnant with the idea of filling the earth. This is the opposite of what Abram was supposed to do. Abram was to go with nothing.

[18]And Noah went forth, and his sons, and his wife, and his sons' wives with him:

Just as Noah departs and obeys so Abram departs but does not fully obey (Gen. 12:4). God told Abram to leave his family, etc. but he disobeys God and takes his father Terah and his nephew Lot.

[19]Every beast, every creeping thing, and every fowl, and whatsoever creepeth upon the earth, after their kinds, went forth out of the ark. [20]And Noah builded an altar unto the LORD; and took of every clean beast, and of every clean fowl, and offered burnt offerings on the altar.

Just as Noah builds an altar unto YHWH so does Abram (Gen. 12:7). There are numerous associations between Noah's altar and the altar Elohim commanded Moses to build on Mt. Horeb and the covenants that followed.

1. The construction of the altars follows a major act of deliverance by the hand of Elohim.

2. The altars and the offerings that follow mark the establishments of a covenant with Elohim (Genesis 9:9, Exodus 24:7).

3. The outcome of both covenants is Elohim's blessing (Genesis 9:1, 23:25).

4. A major provision in both examples is the protection from beasts and enemies (Genesis 9:2-6, 23:22, 29).

5. Both accounts mention that the land will be preserved from destruction (Genesis 9:11, 23:29).

6. Both covenants give conditions which the people must obey (Genesis 9:4, 24:3).

[21]And the LORD smelled a sweet savour; and the LORD said in his heart, I will not again curse the ground any more for man's sake; for the imagination of man's heart is evil from his youth; neither will I again smite any more every thing living, as I have done.

As a result of Noah's offerings the state of mankind before the flood can be restored. An offering on a correctly prescribed altar may yet find Elohim's blessing.

[22]While the earth remaineth, seedtime and harvest, and cold and heat, and summer and winter, and day and night shall not cease.

There are two seasons in Israel, summer and winter, which are summarized in this verse. The early rains (The Feast of Tabernacles) come from September through November, the winter rains from December through February, the latter rains (Passover) through March and April, and dew sustains the plants of the field from May through August. It is summer time and very hot from May (Pentecost) to September and the celebration of Rosh Hashanah (New Years). The plowing and sowing takes place in November and December and barley and wheat are harvested in April and May. An easy way to remember the weather patterns in Israel is high is wet low is dry, west is wet east is dry, north is wet and south is dry.

❧ *Genesis 9* ❧

¹And God blessed Noah and his sons, and said unto them, Be fruitful, and multiply, and replenish the earth.

Just as Elohim blesses Noah and his seed, he blesses Abram and his seed (Gen. 12:2). As we have seen there are numerous parallels between Noah being called out of the ark and Abram being called out of Ur. They both characterize new dispensations and are marked by Elohim's promise of blessing and his endowment of an eternal covenant.

The phrase "And God blessed" is only used within Genesis 1-11 and only applies to Adam and Eve (1:22), the Sabbath (2:3), and Noah. The phrase "And the Lord blessed" is only used in relation to Isaac (26:12), Samson (Judges 13:24), and Obededom who housed the Ark of the Covenant (2 Samuel 6:11).

²And the fear of you and the dread of you shall be upon every beast of the earth, and upon every fowl of the air, upon all that moveth upon the earth, and upon all the fishes of the sea; into your hand are they delivered.

This promise by God is what keeps wolves out of our towns and lions out of our streets and confines them to the wilderness.

³Every moving thing that liveth shall be meat for you; even as the green herb have I given you all things.

Every creature of God is good to eat, and nothing is to be refused by Noah and his sons. Today we are not in the dispensation of the Mosaic Law and thereby under dietary restrictions (Leviticus 11).

⁴But flesh with the life thereof, which is the blood thereof, shall ye not eat.

Man is not to be a riotous eater of flesh. This is because the life of the flesh is in the blood. The blood was what made atonement for their soul. The only record of the Israelites breaking this command was under Saul when they defeated the Philistines and were on the Beth Horon Ridge Route. The people "took sheep, and oxen, and calves, and slew them on the ground: and the people did eat them with the blood…and Saul said, Ye have transgressed: roll a great stone unto me this day" (1 Samuel 14:32-33).

⁵And surely your blood of your lives will I require; at the hand of every beast will I require it, and at the hand of man; at the hand of every man's brother will I require the life of man. ⁶Whoso sheddeth man's blood, by man shall his blood be shed: for in the image of God made he man.

After the flood great attention is given to remind the reader that man is made in the image of God. This is the basis of the model for an eye for an eye. This verse should be viewed as an act of grace that ends the cycle of revenge and limits retaliation.

⁷And you, be ye fruitful, and multiply; bring forth abundantly in the earth, and multiply therein.

There are numerous parallels between Adam and Noah here and throughout the rest of this chapter.

⁸And God spake unto Noah, and to his sons with him, saying, ⁹And I, behold, I establish my covenant with you, and with your seed after you; ¹⁰And with every living creature that is with you, of the fowl, of the cattle, and of every beast of the earth with you; from all that go out of the ark, to every beast of the earth.

Just as YHWH established a covenant with Noah so he does with Abram (Gen. 12:7).

¹¹And I will establish my covenant with you, neither shall all flesh be cut off any more by the waters of a flood; neither shall there any more be a flood to destroy the earth. ¹²And God said, This is the token of the covenant which I make between me and you and every living creature that is with you, for perpetual generations:

The restoration by Elohim was founded on the establishment of a covenant. Let us recall that Elohim may bring other wasting judgments upon the earth for though he bound himself by his promise not to use the arrow of the flood again, he has other arrows of destruction in his quiver.

¹³I do set my bow in the cloud, and it shall be for a token of a covenant between me and the earth. ¹⁴And it shall come to pass, when I bring a cloud over the earth, that the bow shall be seen in the cloud: ¹⁵And I will remember my covenant, which is between me and you and every living creature of all flesh; and the waters shall no more become a flood to destroy all flesh. ¹⁶And the bow shall be in the cloud; and I will look upon it, that I may remember the everlasting covenant between God and every living creature of all flesh that is upon the earth. ¹⁷And God said unto Noah, This is the token of the covenant, which I have established between me and all flesh that is upon the earth.

This is the first of seven tokens mentioned in the Bible, the others are circumcision (17:11), Mount Horeb (Exodus 3:12), the blood on the doorposts (Exodus 12:13), Scripture (Exodus 13:16), Aaron's rod (Numbers 17:10) and the line of scarlet thread in the window at Jericho (Joshua 2:12).

¹⁸And the sons of Noah, that went forth of the ark, were Shem, and Ham, and Japheth: and Ham is the father of Canaan. ¹⁹These are the three sons of Noah: and of them was the whole earth overspread.

See Genesis chapter 10 commentary.

²⁰And Noah began to be an husbandman, and he planted a vineyard:

From here on out is a strikingly different portrait of Noah than that of the pre-flood narrative. Yet this story serves the pen of Moses' purpose because it provides the basis for the end of the Noah story and the state of mankind after the flood…"and he died."

²¹And he drank of the wine, and was drunken; and he was uncovered within his tent.

Notice the similar fruit motif used here and in the garden account with Adam. Noah drank of the fruit and became naked. So we see the parallels between Noah's and Adam's disgrace.

²²And Ham, the father of Canaan, saw the nakedness of his father, and told his two brethren without. ²³And Shem and Japheth took a garment, and laid it upon both their shoulders, and went backward, and covered the nakedness of their father; and their faces were backward, and they saw not their father's nakedness. ²⁴And Noah awoke from his wine, and knew what his younger son had done unto him.

Those who were saved from God's wrath subsequently fell into a form of sin reminiscent of those who died in the judgment and those who later died in Sodom.

²⁵And he said, Cursed be Canaan; a servant of servants shall he be unto his brethren.

Just as Adam's sons were of the seed of the woman or of the seed of the serpent, so Noah's son Ham and his son Canaan continue the line of the seed of the serpent after the flood.

²⁶And he said, Blessed be the LORD God of Shem; and Canaan shall be his servant.

Shem and his line are identified with the seed of the woman.

²⁷God shall enlarge Japheth, and he shall dwell in the tents of Shem; and Canaan shall be his servant.

Japheth and his line are also identified with the seed of the woman.

²⁸And Noah lived after the flood three hundred and fifty years. ²⁹And all the days of Noah were nine hundred and fifty years: and he died.

The phrase "and he died" links chapters five through nine as a literary unit. Moses wants the reader to know that even though Noah was "perfect in his generations" he was a son of Adam and appointed unto death.

❧ *Genesis 10* ❦

¹Now these are the generations of the sons of Noah, Shem, Ham, and Japheth: and unto them were sons born after the flood.

The purpose of Genesis 10 is to provide a historical and geographical description of the land of Canaan (Israel) as the sacred bridge between the ancient civilizations of Egypt and Mesopotamia. The geopolitical situation of Israel was certainly impressed upon the minds of the ancients, and Moses describes the land through a genealogy of the inhabitants in and around Israel. The roster is a survey of mostly Gentilic nations, 70 in number (the number 70 representing the number of totality, in Job 38-40 the Lord asks Job 70 questions, forgive 70 times 7 is required in Matthew 18:22). The chapter is a genealogical tree, working in the form of a pyramid from the top down, starting with the three sons of Noah; Shem, Ham and Japheteh.

The sons of Shem settled to the east of the land of Israel and were the closest related to the Israelites, the sons of Ham to the south, and the sons of Japheteh to the north and northwest. The order followed in the chapter is political and territorial, as well as being divided by their ethnicity and language, the sons of Noah and their sons are allotted homelands by God. The people of the world were placed in their respective lands by God who established their borders but Elohim kept one land for himself, Israel.

²The sons of Japheth; Gomer, and Magog, and Madai, and Javan, and Tubal, and Meshech, and Tiras.

The sons of Japheteh settled on the outermost fringes of the known world in the eastern Mediterranean Sea. The sons of Japheteh were the progenitors of the Greek and Pre-Greek nations. Gomer the father of the Celtic family, Magog in Russia, Madai the Medes, Javan in Greece, Tubal in Anatolia around the Black Sea, Mesheceh in Anatolia, and Tiras, the progenitor of the Thracians.

³And the sons of Gomer; Ashkenaz, and Riphath, and Togarmah. ⁴And the sons of Javan; Elishah, and Tarshish, Kittim, and Dodanim. ⁵By these were the isles of the Gentiles divided in their lands; every one after his tongue, after their families, in their nations.

The next generation of the sons of Japheteh continued to expand their territory; the son of Gomer, Ashkenaz dwelt in modern day Germany, and the sons of Javan; Elishah in Cyprus, Tarshish in Tarshish, Kittim in Crete, and Dodanim in Rhodes. The sons of Japheteh were of an Indo-European dialect.

⁶And the sons of Ham; Cush, and Mizraim, and Phut, and Canaan.

The second group contains the sons of Ham, which were Semitic despite their allegiance to Egypt.

To the sons of Ham belong Canaanites (the seed of the serpent) such as the Jebusites, Amorites, and Girgashties. Even the Philistines who settled in the southern coastal plain were considered in the orbit of the sphere of Egyptian influence.

⁷And the sons of Cush; Seba, and Havilah, and Sabtah, and Raamah, and Sabtechah: and the sons of Raamah; Sheba, and Dedan. ⁸And Cush begat Nimrod: he began to be a mighty one in the earth. ⁹He was a mighty hunter before the LORD: wherefore it is said, Even as Nimrod the mighty hunter before the LORD. ¹⁰And the beginning of his kingdom was Babel, and Erech, and Accad, and Calneh, in the land of Shinar. ¹¹Out of that land went forth Asshur, and builded Nineveh, and the city Rehoboth, and Calah, ¹²And Resen between Nineveh and Calah: the same is a great city. ¹³And Mizraim begat Ludim, and Anamim, and Lehabim, and Naphtuhim, ¹⁴And Pathrusim, and Casluhim, (out of whom came Philistim,) and Caphtorim. ¹⁵And Canaan begat Sidon his first born, and Heth, ¹⁶And the Jebusite, and the Amorite, and the Girgasite, ¹⁷And the Hivite, and the Arkite, and the Sinite, ¹⁸And the Arvadite, and the Zemarite, and the Hamathite: and afterward were the families of the Canaanites spread abroad.

The descendants of Ham, Seba, Havilah, Sheba, and Dedan settled in the South Arabia region but had a close affinity to Africa. Though Asshur is included in the genealogy of the sons of Shem, Nimrod was the progenitor of settlements in Assyria between the Euphrates and Tigris rivers. Nimrod founded cities in southern Mesopotamia in Babel, Erech, Accad, and Calneh. In northern Mesopotamia he founded cities in Nineveh, Rehoboth, and Calah.

¹⁹And the border of the Canaanites was from Sidon, as thou comest to Gerar, unto Gaza; as thou goest, unto Sodom, and Gomorrah, and Admah, and Zeboim, even unto Lasha. ²⁰These are the sons of Ham, after their families, after their tongues, in their countries, and in their nations.

The borders of the land of Canaan are given in the allotment to the sons of Ham. The border starts at the Phoenician coastal city of Sidon, traverses south through the Plain of Acco, the Sharon Plain, and the Coastal Plain to the port city of Gaza, the "strong city," which was the most important and closest city in the Land of Israel to Egypt. The border continues from Gaza east to the cities of the plain, Sodom, and Gomorrah, which are traditionally located at the southern end of the Dead Sea. The border continued north to Lasha (Dan) and did not include any of Transjordan.

²¹Unto Shem also, the father of all the children of Eber, the brother of Japheth the elder, even to him were children born.

The sons of Shem were speakers of a northwest Semitic dialect and did not inhabit any of the regions of Transjordan. The third group contains the sons of Shem, which were the closest related to the Israelites, through Joktan the father of Eber.

²²The children of Shem; Elam, and Asshur, and Arphaxad, and Lud, and Aram. ²³And the children of Aram; Uz, and Hul, and Gether, and Mash. ²⁴And Arphaxad begat Salah; and Salah begat Eber.

Besides Elam who settled in southern Persia, and Lud who settled in Asia Minor, the sons of Shem inhabited three different regions to the east of the Land of Israel. Asshur and his sons settled in Mesopotamia, Aram and his sons settled in northern Mesopotamia, along the Fertile Crescent to Syria and into northern Transjordan, and the sons of Joktan settled in the region around South Arabia.

[25]And unto Eber were born two sons: the name of one was Peleg; for in his days was the earth divided; and his brother's name was Joktan.[26]And Joktan begat Almodad, and Sheleph, and Hazarmaveth, and Jerah, [27]And Hadoram, and Uzal, and Diklah, [28]And Obal, and Abimael, and Sheba, [29]And Ophir, and Havilah, and Jobab: all these were the sons of Joktan. [30]And their dwelling was from Mesha, as thou goest unto Sephar a mount of the east. [31]These are the sons of Shem, after their families, after their tongues, in their lands, after their nations. [32]These are the families of the sons of Noah, after their generations, in their nations: and by these were the nations divided in the earth after the flood.

The survey is to show the sphere of influence of the three sons of Noah and to identify how they settled to the south, east, north, and northwest of Israel. The purpose of the chapter is to show how all of humanity is connected to and came from the Promise Land.

❧ Genesis 11 ❧

¹And the whole earth was of one language, and of one speech.

This verse and verse four indicate that the sons of Noah were not filling the earth as they were commanded but were clustered together in and around the southern end of the Fertile Crescent.

²And it came to pass, as they journeyed from the east, that they found a plain in the land of Shinar; and they dwelt there.

Again we have the geographical term east associated with impending judgment. The sons of Noah are at first pictured as sojourners who finally settled in the land between the rivers. These sons of Noah started an unholy construction in a plain in Shinar (Babylon) like Nebuchadnezzar later built his unholy statue in a plain in Babylon. Shinar is here first recognized as the mother or seat of all spiritual harlotry and abominations.

³And they said one to another, Go to, let us make brick, and burn them thoroughly. And they had brick for stone, and slime had they for morter.

The mud would be gathered from the banks of the Tigris and Euphrates Rivers and molded into sun dried bricks. The slime was bituminous asphalt and imported from places like the Dead Sea.

⁴And they said, Go to, let us build us a city and a tower, whose top may reach unto heaven; and let us make us a name, lest we be scattered abroad upon the face of the whole earth.

Their reason for building the city and the tower was to make them famous, to give them a name (Shem), and to provide them a city to dwell in so they would not have to fill the earth.

⁵And the LORD came down to see the city and the tower, which the children of men builded.

The further we read in the early chapters of Genesis, the further the LORD's fellowship with man in a physical form is removed. At first he walked with man in the garden, now he is transcendent in the third heaven.

⁶And the LORD said, Behold, the people is one, and they have all one language; and this they begin to do: and now nothing will be restrained from them, which they have imagined to do. ⁷Go to, let us go down, and there confound their language, that they may not understand one another's speech. ⁸So the LORD scattered them abroad from thence upon the face of all the earth: and they left off to build the city. ⁹Therefore is the name of it called Babel; because the LORD did there confound the language of all the earth: and from thence did the LORD scatter them abroad upon the face of all the earth.

The fact that they left off to build the city and the tower that reaches unto heaven implies that it will be finished one day in the future.

Made in the USA
Middletown, DE
18 March 2015